A New True Book

KENNEDY SPACE CENTER

By Timothy R. Gaffney

CHILDRENS PRESS ®

CHICAGO

Artist's drawing of what a space
station might look like.

PHOTO CREDITS

JFK Space Center—2, 4, 10, 18, 26, 30,
32, 35, 41

NASA—Cover, 8, 9, 13 (left), 23 (left), 33,
34 (2 photos), 36, 37 (left), 38 (left), 40,
42, 43, 44

National Air and Space Museum—12
(2 photos), 13 (right), 23 (right), 38 (right)

U.S. Fish and Wildlife Service—15, 16

Sovfoto—20 (right), 24

Jet Propulsion Laboratory—20 (left)

Finley-Holiday Films—29, 37 (right)

Len Meents—7

COVER—Huge crawler carries space
shuttle and its rocket to the launchpad.

Library of Congress Cataloging in Publication Data

Gaffney, Timothy R.
  Kennedy Space Center.

  (A New true book)
  Includes index
  Summary: Describes the history and work of the
John F. Kennedy Space Center located on Merritt Island
on the east coast of Florida.
    1. John F. Kennedy Space Center—Juvenile literature.
[1. John F. Kennedy Space Center. 2. Space flight]
I. Title. II. Series. A new true book.
TL4027.F52J638 1985   629.47'8'0975927   85-11317
ISBN 0-516-01269-X   AACR2

TABLE OF CONTENTS

BLAST-OFF

It is a quiet morning on Merritt Island in Florida. Sunlight gleams on marshes and ponds. Near the seashore, a tall rocket sits on a raised concrete pad.

The rocket breaks the stillness with a mighty roar. Flames leap from its engines. Seconds later, the rocket climbs into the sky, leaving a trail of smoke.

MERRITT ISLAND

Merritt Island is the home of the John F. Kennedy Space Center. It is where America launches astronauts into space.

Kennedy Space Center is located along the east coast of Florida. The water between Merritt Island and the coast is called the Indian River. Beyond Merritt Island is the Atlantic Ocean.

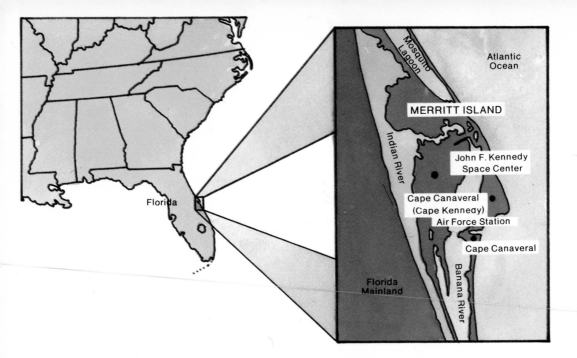

Just to the south of Merritt Island is Cape Canaveral and the Cape Canaveral Air Force Station. The space center was once on Cape Canaveral. The first American astronauts took off from there.

The *Columbia* was America's first space shuttle.

Rockets are still launched from Cape Canaveral. But space shuttles take off from Merritt Island. A space

shuttle is a rocket with
wings like an airplane.
Space shuttles also can
land on Merritt Island, on a
special runway.

Discovery glides to a landing.

SPACE SHUTTLES AND SATELLITES

Kennedy Space Center has launched many satellites into orbit. Anything that circles the earth without falling out of space is called a satellite. A satellite is in orbit when it is circling the earth.

Some satellites ride into orbit in space shuttles. And some space shuttles have

11

The *Mariner 2* satellite (above) sent
back pictures of Venus in 1962.
Mariner 10 (right) photographed
Venus and Mercury in 1973.

brought satellites back
from orbit to the space
center.

Kennedy Space Center
has launched many
spaceships to the moon
and to other planets. Years

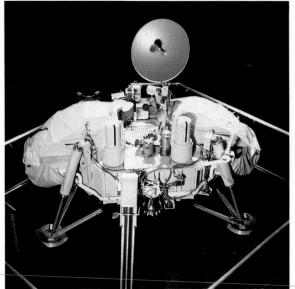

Lunar modules (left) landed astronauts on the moon. A *Viking* satellite traveled to Mars in 1976.

ago, astronauts landed on the moon and explored parts of it. Spaceships controlled from Earth have landed on Mars. Others have flown past the planets Mercury, Venus, Jupiter, and Saturn.

13

WILDLIFE AND HISTORY

Merritt Island is home to more than just spaceships. Much of it is a wildlife refuge. Many rare animals live on the island's beaches, or in its saltwater marshes and ponds.

Pelicans, bald eagles, and manatees (sea cows) are a few of the rare animals that live there. Alligators live there, too.

Flocks of birds nest on Merritt Island.

Tribes of Native Americans were the first people on Merritt Island and Cape Canaveral. They hunted and fished there thousands of years ago. There are still mounds of earth where they buried their dead, and piles of

15

shells from the shellfish
they ate.

Explorers from Spain
gave Cape Canaveral its
name more than four
hundred years ago. They
noticed fields of sugarcane
growing there and gave it
a Spanish name that
means "cane field."

FIRST FLIGHT
FROM THE CAPE

Rockets are launched
from concrete launchpads.
The United States Air
Force began building the
first launchpad on Cape
Canaveral in 1949. It
launched its first rocket
there on July 24, 1950.

The air force tested new
rockets by launching them

Aerial view of launchpad at the Kennedy Space Center

over the ocean. That is the safest way to test rockets. Ships are warned to stay away when rockets are launched.

THE SPACE RACE

In the 1950s, America
and Russia both were
testing rockets. The tests
turned into a race. Which
nation would be the first to
put a satellite in orbit?
Which would be the first to
send a person into space?

Russia launched the first
satellite, *Sputnik 1,* on
October 4, 1957.

The United States tried
to launch its first satellite

A Jupiter rocket (left) carried *Explorer 1* into orbit. Russia's *Sputnik 1* (above) was the first satellite in space.

on December 6, 1957. The rocket rose three feet. Then it fell back on its pad and exploded. The U.S. Army finally put a small satellite named *Explorer 1* into orbit on January 31, 1958.

BIRTH OF NASA

The National Aeronautics and Space Administration (NASA) came into being on October 1, 1958. NASA was put in charge of America's space programs. NASA set up its space center at Cape Canaveral.

In December 1958, NASA told of its plan to send a man into space. It called this plan Project Mercury. The *Mercury* spaceship would be a little capsule shaped like a bell. Only one astronaut could fit into it at a time.

A rocket would shoot the capsule into space. Then small rockets on the capsule would slow it down. It would land on the ocean with the help of parachutes.

But Russia was first again. On April 12, 1961, Yuri A. Gagarin became the first man in space. He

Astronaut Alan B. Shepard, Jr. (left)
orbited the earth in *Freedom 7* (above).

circled the earth once in a
space capsule, *Vostok 1.*
America launched its
first space traveler on
May 5, 1961. His name
was Alan B. Shepard, Jr.
He traveled 302 miles in

Cosmonaut Yuri Gagarin was the first human to orbit the earth.

15 minutes. It was a good
flight. But it was not as
exciting as Russia's.
Americans felt they were
losing the space race.

A NEW PLAN

On May 25, 1961,
President John F. Kennedy
told Americans about a
new space plan. He said:

> I believe that this nation
> should commit itself to
> achieving the goal, before this
> decade is out, of landing a
> man on the moon and
> returning him safely to earth.

America would need a
big, new rocket and a new
spaceship to send a man
to the moon. And it would

The National Aeronautics and Space Administration space center

need a new space center
to launch the rocket.

Cape Canaveral had no
room left for such big
rockets. NASA decided to
build a new space center
on Merritt Island.

PROJECT APOLLO

NASA called its moon plan Project Apollo. First there would be several *Apollo* test flights. Then an *Apollo* capsule would carry three astronauts into orbit around the moon and bring them back to earth.

From the capsule NASA would launch an *Apollo* spaceship called the lunar module. The lunar module would land on the moon with two of the astronauts from the capsule.

Both spaceships would ride into space on a *Saturn 5* rocket. The *Saturn 5* would stand as tall as a thirty-six-story building. It would be the most powerful rocket ever built.

The new space center would have to be huge to handle such big rockets. The moon rockets would

Huge crawlers carry the space shuttle
and its rocket to its launchpad.

be put together in a
building called the Vehicle
Assembly Building. A
crawler as big as a house
would move the rocket to
a launchpad. The
launchpads would be more

29

Crawler moves toward the launchpads.

than three miles from the control center. This would keep people in the center safe from the blast of the rocket engines.

THE DOOR TO THE MOON

It took thousands of workers five years to build the new space center. President John F. Kennedy never lived to see it. He was shot to death on November 22, 1963. The space center was named in his memory.

The morning of May 21, 1969, came at last. The Vehicle Assembly Building opened one of its great

Apollo 11 sits
on top of the
Saturn 5 rocket.

doors. Inside stood a
Saturn 5 rocket. High on
top of the rocket sat the
lunar capsule *Apollo 11.*

A crane lifts the *Apollo* spacecraft.

The crawler inched the rocket forward on four pairs of tracks. The crawler had to creep along to keep the rocket steady. Slowly it made its way three-and-a-half miles to the launchpad. The trip took seven hours.

The *Saturn 5* rocket lifts off (left). The *Apollo* command and service module (right) orbited the moon.

THE FIRST MOON LANDING

Apollo 11 blasted off on July 16, 1969. Four days later, astronaut Michael Collins circled the moon in

The earth rises over the moon's horizon.

the capsule while the other
two astronauts, Neil
Armstrong and Edwin
Aldrin, Jr., flew down to the
moon's surface in the lunar
module. Neil Armstrong
became the first man to
set foot on the moon. They

Close-up of
the lunar
module on
the moon

all got back safely. They
brought rocks from the
moon with them.

The space center
launched six more flights
to the moon over the next
three years.

SKYLAB AND SOYUZ

On May 14, 1973, a
Saturn 5 carried a
different kind of spaceship.
It was a space station
named *Skylab*. *Skylab* was
a place where three

Skylab (left) and *Soyuz* (right) met in space.

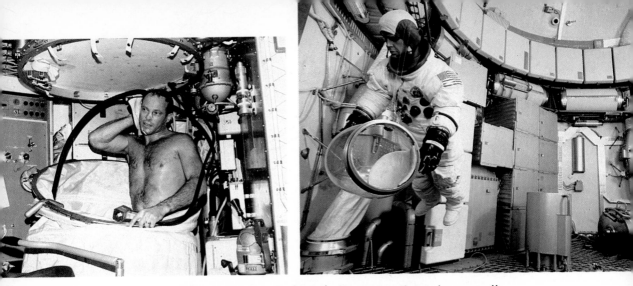

The interior of *Skylab*'s science lab (right). Because there is no pull of gravity in orbit, everything used in space must be tied down or contained in some way. Astronaut Jack R. Lousma (above) used a vacuum to collect water left over from his space shower.

astronauts could live for weeks while they circled the earth. It had much more room than a capsule.

Three different crews flew up to *Skylab* in *Apollo* capsules. The first crew stayed for twenty-eight days. The second

crew stayed for fifty-nine
days. The third crew
stayed for eighty-four
days—almost three months!

Nobody visited *Skylab*
after that. The space
station's orbit drifted lower
and lower. Finally *Skylab*
fell back to earth. Most of
it burned up like a meteor.

Americans and Russians
met in space on July 15,
1975. The meeting was
carefully planned. A
Russian *Soyuz* spaceship

Astronaut Thomas P. Stafford (top) greets Cosmonaut Aleksey A. Leonov.

and an American *Apollo* capsule joined together. The two-man Russian crew and three-man American crew visited each other for two days. Then they separated and landed in their own capsules.

THE FUTURE

The Kennedy Space
Center—first built for moon
rockets—is now used for
space shuttles. The
shuttles are attached to
their booster rockets in the

Vehicle Assembly Building.
The same crawlers move
them to the launchpad.
In coming years, space
shuttles will carry parts of

Future space stations will have living quarters and factories.
Someday products made in space will be sold on earth.

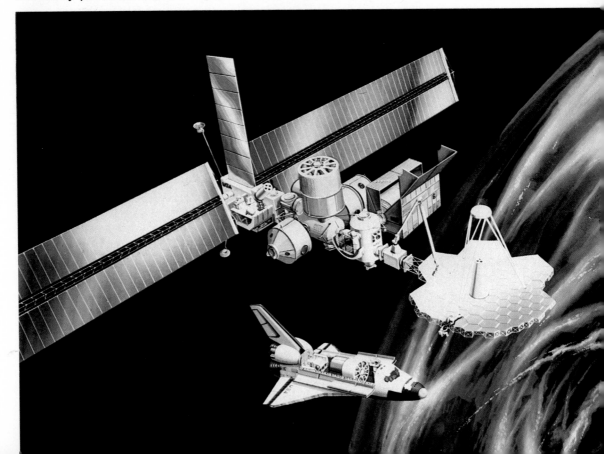

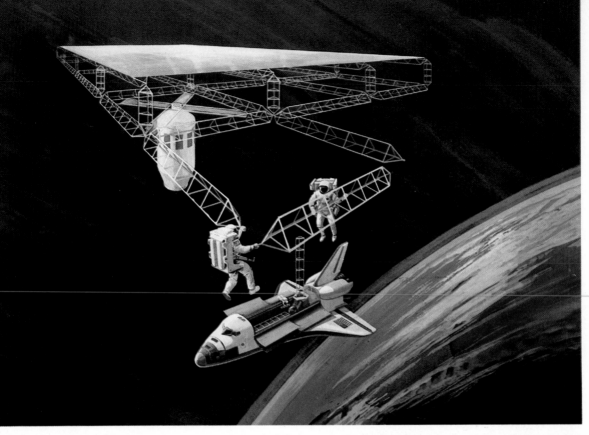

Astronauts, wearing manned maneuvering units, will be able to build space platforms.

a space station into orbit. Astronauts will put the space station together. It will have room for more astronauts than *Skylab* held.

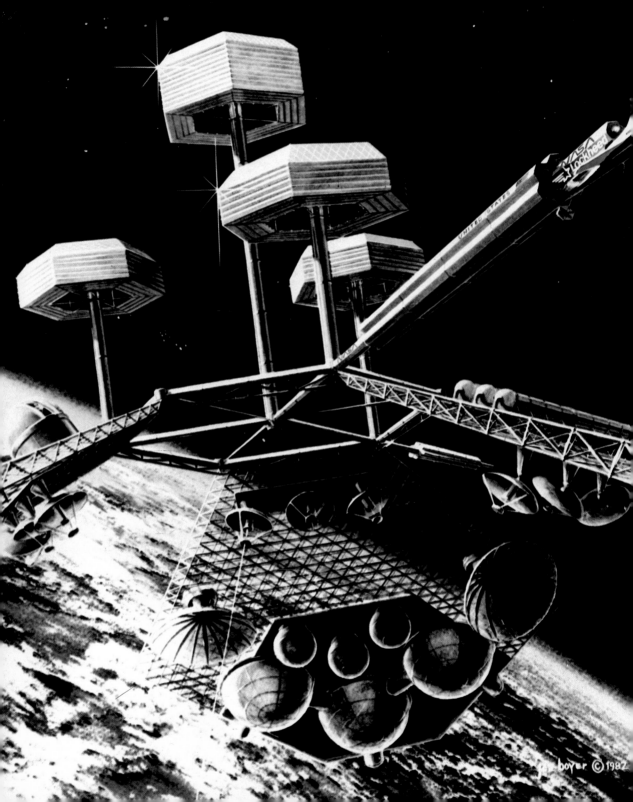

The space station will be
a place where scientists
can study the earth and
space for weeks or
months. It may become a
place where spaceships
pick up fuel on their way
to the moon or Mars.

Space shuttles and the
space station will keep
Kennedy Space Center
busy for years to come.

WORDS YOU SHOULD KNOW

astronauts(AST • roh • nawts)—American space travelers

booster rocket(BOO • ster ROCK • et)—an initial rocket stage that boosts (that is, lifts or pushes) a spacecraft into flight

capsule(KAP • sul)—a small enclosed spaceship

crawler(KRAWL • er)—a huge vehicle that moves slowly on chain tracks to carry rockets and spaceships from an assembly building to a launchpad

launchpad(LAWNCH • pad)—a concrete platform or surface from which rockets or other spaceships are launched

lunar(LOON • er)—pertaining to the moon

meteor(MEET • ee • er)—a small piece of space matter that becomes visible when it burns up as it falls into the earth's atmosphere

module(MAWJ • yool)—a separate unit that is part of a spaceship

orbit(OR • bit)—the path an object takes as it moves around another object

satellite(SAT • ul • eyet)—a man-made object that orbits the earth without falling from space

shuttle(SHUT • til)—a vehicle that carries cargo or people over a prearranged route

Skylab(SKY • lab)—an orbiting space laboratory, large enough to carry several crew members

space station(SPAISS STAY • shun)—an artificial satellite on which people can live and work

INDEX

About the author

Timothy R. Gaffney is a staff feature writer for the Dayton Daily News *and the* Journal Herald, *publications of Dayton Newspapers, Inc. He has won state awards for feature writing from the Ohio Associated Press, the Ohio Newspaper Women's Association, and the Ohio Public Images Association. He lives in Miamisburg, Ohio, with his wife, Jean, and his daughter, Kimberly.*